INSECT WORLD

MOSQUITOES

SANDRA MARKLE

TINY INSECT TROUBLEMAKERS

⌐ LERNER PUBLICATIONS COMPANY MINNEAPOLIS

FOR CURIOUS KIDS EVERYWHERE

ACKNOWLEDGMENTS

The author would like to thank Dr. Donald Barnard, USDA-ARS Center for Medical, Agricultural, and Veterinary Entomology, in Gainesville, Florida; and Dr. Gregory Lanzaro, Director of the U.C. Mosquito Research Program at the University of California, Davis; and Dr. Elizabeth Willott, Entomology Department at the University of Arizona, for sharing their expertise and enthusiasm. The author would also like to thank Dr. Simon Pollard, Curator of Invertebrate Zoology at Canterbury Museum, Christchurch, New Zealand, for his help with the scientific name pronunciation guides. Finally, a special thanks to Skip Jeffery, who shared the effort and joy of creating this book.

Lerner Publications Company
A division of Lerner Publishing Group, Inc.
241 First Avenue North
Minneapolis, MN 55401

Website address: www.lernerbooks.com

Library of Congress Cataloging-in-Publication Data

Markle, Sandra.
     Mosquitoes : tiny insect troublemakers / by Sandra Markle.
       p.   cm. — (Insect world)
     Includes bibliographical references and index.
     ISBN 978–0–8225–7299–2 (lib. bdg. : alk. paper)
     1. Mosquitoes—Juvenile literature. I. Title.
QL536.M214 2008
595.77′2–dc22   2007025264

Manufactured in the United States of America
1 2 3 4 5 6 – DP – 13 12 11 10 09 08

CONTENTS

INSECT WORLD

WELCOME TO THE WORLD OF INSECTS—

those animals nicknamed bugs. It truly is the insects' world. Scientists have discovered more than a million different kinds—more than any other kind of animal. And they are everywhere—even on the frozen continent of Antarctica.

So how can you tell if what you see is an insect, rather than a relative, like a crab (*below*)? Both belong to a group of animals called arthropods (AR-throh-podz). The animals in this group share some features. They have bodies divided into segments, jointed legs, and a stiff exoskeleton. This is a skeleton on the outside like a suit of armor. But the one sure way to tell if an animal is an insect is to count its legs. All adult insects have six legs. They're the only animals in the world with six legs.

This book is about mosquitoes. Female mosquitoes bite animals and people to get a meal of blood. Sometimes when they bite, they spread diseases. Then mosquitoes become real insect troublemakers.

MOSQUITO FACT

Like all insects, a mosquito's body temperature rises and falls with the temperature around it. They must warm up to be active.

ON THE OUTSIDE

Take a look at this adult female mosquito. If you could touch it, its body would feel like tough plastic. Instead of having a hard, bony skeleton inside the way you do, an insect has an exoskeleton. This hard coat covers its whole body—even its eyes. The exoskeleton is made up of separate plates connected by stretchy tissue. This lets it bend and move. Check out the other key parts that all mosquitoes share.

ANTENNA: This is one of a pair of movable feelers. Hairs on the antennae sense chemical for smells.

HEAD

THORAX

COMPOUND EYES: What look like big eyes are really hundreds of eye units packed together. These let the insect look in every direction at once.

PROBOSCIS: This mouthpart is made up of a tube and cutting blades. The mouth opening is at the tip. It is used for sucking in blood and plant juices. It also injects saliva.

6

HALTERES:
These are clublike growths in place of hind wings. They help with balance and steering. The wings and halteres are attached to the thorax.

WINGS:
Mosquitoes have two see-through wings. They are fringed with scales.

ABDOMEN

SPIRACLES:
These holes down the sides of the thorax and abdomen let air into and out of the body for breathing.

LEGS AND FEET:
These are used for walking and holding on. Mosquito legs are long and thin so the mosquito can land gently and go unnoticed. All legs are attached to the thorax.

ON THE INSIDE

Now, look inside an adult female mosquito.

HEART: This muscular tube pumps blood toward the head. Then the blood flows throughout the body.

BRAIN: This receives messages from the antennae, eyes, and sensory hairs. It sends signals to control all body parts.

PHARYNX: Food passes through this tube. The tube stretches through the proboscis to where it joins the esophagus.

ESOPHAGUS: Food passes through this tube between the pharynx and the crop and stomach.

SALIVARY GLAND: This gland produces saliva for digestion. Saliva is spit. In females, the saliva contains a chemical to keep blood from clotting.

Approved by Dr. Elizabeth Willott, University of Arizona

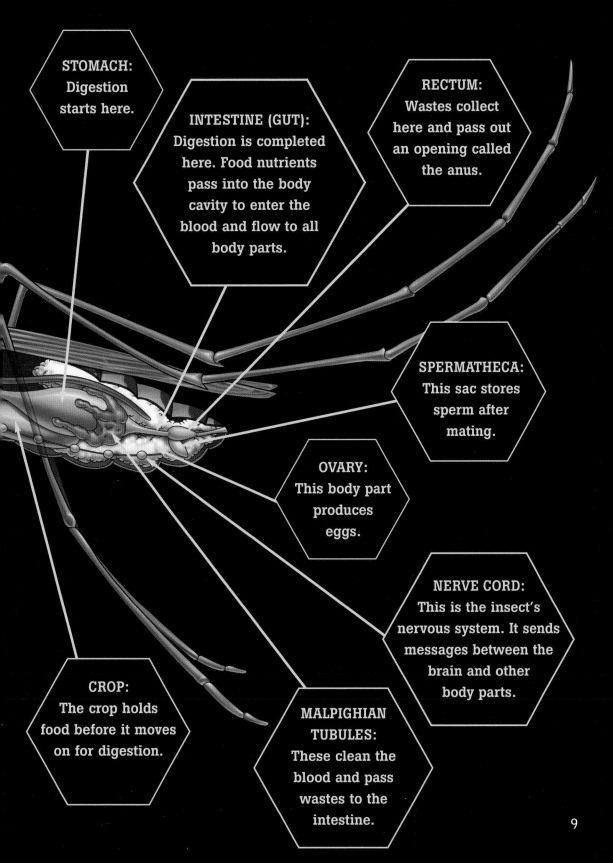

STOMACH: Digestion starts here.

INTESTINE (GUT): Digestion is completed here. Food nutrients pass into the body cavity to enter the blood and flow to all body parts.

RECTUM: Wastes collect here and pass out an opening called the anus.

SPERMATHECA: This sac stores sperm after mating.

OVARY: This body part produces eggs.

NERVE CORD: This is the insect's nervous system. It sends messages between the brain and other body parts.

CROP: The crop holds food before it moves on for digestion.

MALPIGHIAN TUBULES: These clean the blood and pass wastes to the intestine.

9

BECOMING AN ADULT

Insect babies grow into adults in two ways: complete metamorphosis (me-teh-MOR-feh-sus) and incomplete metamorphosis. Metamorphosis means change. Mosquitoes develop through complete metamorphosis. Their life includes four stages: egg, larva, pupa, and adult. See how different the mosquito looks during each stage of its life. It behaves very differently too.

IN INCOMPLETE METAMORPHOSIS, insects go through three stages: egg, nymph, and adult. Nymphs are much like small adults. But nymphs can't reproduce.

CULEX MOSQUITO EGGS

Mosquito larvae live in ponds or even puddles. They eat tiny plants and bacteria. They don't bother people. When the larvae become adults and fly away, they feed on plant juices. Then they pair up and mate. After mating, the females of most kinds of mosquitoes seek out animals and people to bite. They need the energy they get from a blood meal to produce eggs. The bites form annoying, itchy welts. But mosquito bites can also spread diseases that make people sick or even kill them. That's why mosquitoes are public enemies.

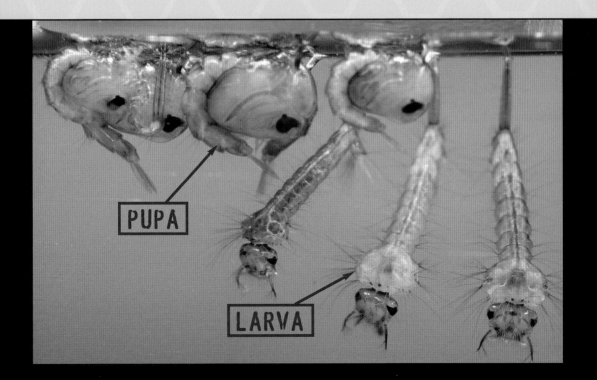

PUPA

LARVA

FIRST BITE

It's late on a warm May afternoon when the young female *Anopheles* (eh-NAW-feh-lez) mosquito takes flight. She lands on a flower. Then she feeds on the sweet liquid, called nectar, the flower produces.

As the sun sets, she flies again. Soon she joins a swarm of mosquitoes. She zips this way and that until she finds a mate. The male inserts a packet of his sperm into her body. It will be stored there until she's ready to produce eggs.

MOSQUITO FACT

Different kinds of mosquitoes beat their wings at different speeds. The faster the beat, the higher pitched the buzz. Mosquitoes find mates by homing in on just the right buzz.

That night and all the next day, the female mosquito rests. Then, in the evening, she sets off on her first search flight. She is tracking down a meal of blood. The female can sense tiny amounts of carbon dioxide in the air. Animals give off this gas when they breathe. She follows this gas trail and homes in on a group of people. She selects one of them to bite.

MOSQUITO FACT

Male mosquitoes don't have mouthparts for piercing skin. They only suck plant juices.

The female sucks blood with her proboscis. This long, strawlike mouthpart has sharp parts to pierce skin. The mosquito pokes her proboscis through a person's skin and into a capillary. This is a small blood vessel. She does this so quickly and easily that the person may not even notice. Then the female mosquito spits out a little saliva, the juice in her mouth. Her saliva contains a chemical that keeps the blood cells in the capillary from sticking together. This makes it easier for her to suck in a blood meal.

MOSQUITO FACT

Mosquito bites itch because humans have an allergic reaction to mosquito saliva.

PARASITE ON BOARD

After her meal, the female *Anopheles* flies to a nearby plant. She rests while her eggs develop. But something else is also developing inside her. Because the person she bit was sick, her blood meal contained tiny living things called *Plasmodium vivax* (plaz–MOH–dee–um VEYE–vax). These are parasites. Parasites are living things that live in or on animals or people, their host. They get the food they need from their host. They may make their host sick. *Plasmodium* parasites cause people to have fevers, chills, headaches, muscle pains, and stomach pains. People call this illness malaria.

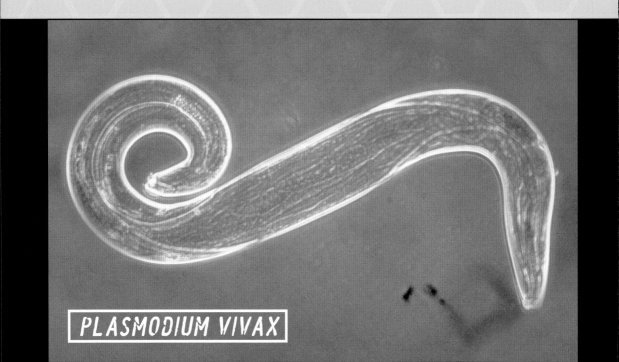

PLASMODIUM VIVAX

The *Plasmodium* parasites do not make the female mosquito sick, though. Inside her, the parasites simply continue their life cycle. Male and female *Plasmodium* mate. They produce cells that contain thousands of little organisms called sporozoites (spo-ro-ZOH-eyetz). These burst out of the cells and travel through the mosquito's body to the salivary gland. This is the body part where her saliva is made.

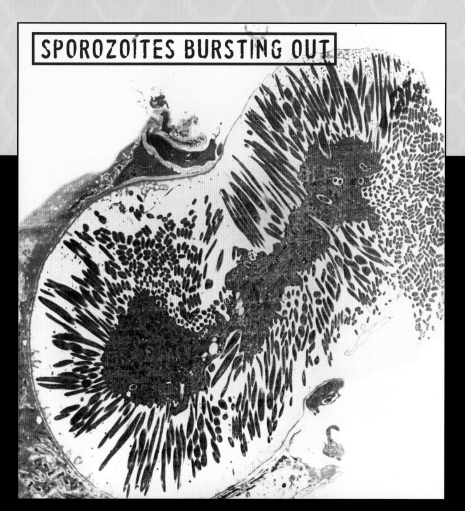

SPOROZOITES BURSTING OUT

The female mosquito is ready to lay her eggs. She sips flower nectar for energy to fly. Then she goes searching for water. When she finds a small pond, she lands on the surface. There the female *Anopheles* lays her eggs one at a time. *Anopheles* eggs are unique. They have winglike parts to keep them afloat. The female lays nearly two hundred eggs in all. Then she flies off in search of another blood meal.

MOSQUITO FACT

In tropical climates, the eggs may hatch in a few days. In colder climates, they take as long as three weeks to hatch.

SECOND BITE

When the female mosquito bites another person, she spits out a little of her saliva again. When she does, she also spits out some of the sporozoites. The mosquito gets the blood she needs and flies away. The *Plasmodium* parasites now continue their life cycle inside the person who was bitten. This is their new host. First, they attack the host's liver. Then they attack the host's red blood cells. When they do this, the person gets sick. The person suffers with a fever, chills, and all the other malaria symptoms. Not every female *Anopheles* mosquito spreads malaria when it bites. However, in tropical countries, many do.

MOSQUITO FACT

More than 600 million people suffer from malaria each year. Between 1 and 3 million people a year die from this disease.

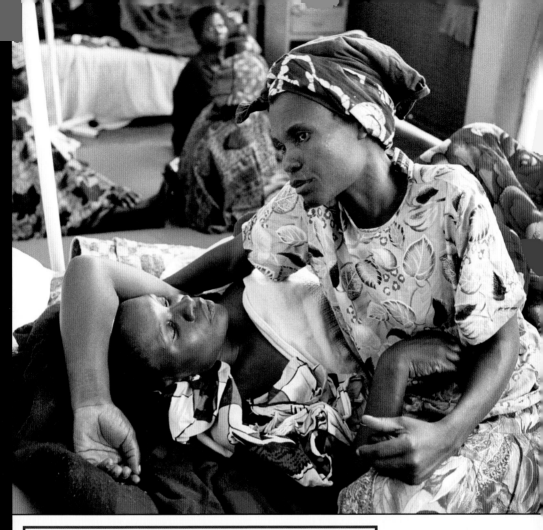

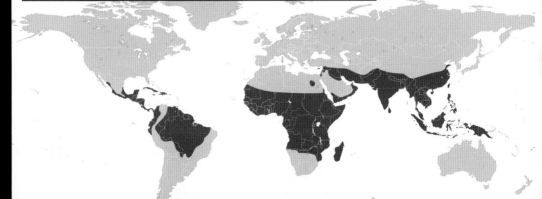

PLACES WHERE MALARIA IS FOUND

LARVAE AND PUPAE

LARVA STAGE

The female *Anopheles* mosquito laid her eggs on the surface of a small pond. When the larvae hatch, they jerk their bodies to dive underwater. There they feed on any algae or bacteria they find before surfacing again. In between dives, the larvae rest at the surface. They breathe by taking in air through the spiracles that are above water.

Day after day, the mosquito larvae continue to eat and grow. They grow too big for their exoskeletons. Then they molt. Their armorlike coverings split open along the back, and they wiggle out. There is already a new protective coat underneath. It is soft and flexible at first, letting the mosquito stretch and gain room to grow bigger. For about two weeks, the larvae continue to grow and molt. As the larvae get ready for the fourth and final molt, their bodies change. This time when their exoskeletons split open, the pupae emerge.

MOSQUITO FACT

The larvae of most other kinds of mosquitoes have tubes for breathing.

PUPA STAGE

Like the larvae, the *Anopheles* pupae have a hard exoskeleton. But the pupae don't feed or pass wastes. If they are disturbed, they jerk and dive by tumbling down through the water. Then they pop back up to the surface again. They have two tubes for breathing air. While the pupae seem to be resting at the surface, inside a lot is going on. The old larval body parts are breaking down. New adult body parts are forming. After a few days, the process is complete. Then the pupae split open along the back, and the adults crawl out.

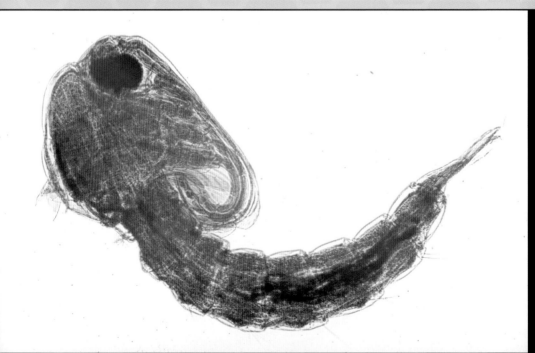

MOSQUITOES AND DISEASE

Malaria is just one of the diseases mosquitoes spread. Yellow fever is another. Its symptoms are similar to those for malaria. However, it also causes infected people's eyes to turn yellow. That's how this disease got its name. Yellow fever is usually spread by *Aedes* (a–EE–deez) mosquitoes. They can be identified by the black stripes on their bodies and legs.

MOSQUITO FACT

Africa, Central and South America, and the islands of the Caribbean have the most cases of yellow fever.

PLACES WHERE YELLOW FEVER IS FOUND

Female *Aedes* mosquitoes spread yellow fever when they feed on people or animals. The males, like the one shown below feeding on a pear, live on plant juices.

FEMALE

MALE

Aedes mosquitoes are unique in where they choose to lay their eggs. Instead of in water, they lay them on damp soil. This is often soil along streams or fields that are flooded to irrigate plants, like rice. About two days after the eggs are covered with water, the larvae hatch. Then the larvae grow up in water.

MOSQUITO FACT

Aedes eggs can survive dry conditions for up to nine months.

DENGUE FEVER

There are a number of different kinds of *Aedes* mosquitoes. One kind, called the Asian tiger mosquito, is noted for spreading dengue (DEN-gee) fever.

MOSQUITO FACT

Asian tiger mosquitoes get their name from their tigerlike striped legs and bands of white spots on their bodies.

A microphotograph can show objects smaller than the eye can see. This microphotograph is of the tiny living things that cause dengue fever. These organisms are a kind of virus. The virus can live inside the Asian tiger mosquito and is carried from person to person when the mosquito bites. It may be hard to believe that such a little thing could make people sick. Dengue fever is sometimes called breakbone fever. It's called that because people with this disease have terrible pains in their joints.

MOSQUITO FACT

There are many cases of dengue fever each year in Africa, China, India, the Middle East, the Caribbean, Central and South America, Australia, and the South Pacific islands.

PLACES WHERE DENGUE FEVER IS FOUND

Asian tiger mosquitoes are puddle and container breeders. That means the larvae can grow up in small amounts of water. The adults are weak fliers and are unable to travel very far at a time. In fact, in their whole lifetime, these mosquitoes rarely fly farther than 200 yards (182 meters). They live and breed close to the people the females bite. Unlike most other mosquitoes, Asian tiger mosquitoes fly and bite during the day.

MOSQUITO FACT

The U.S. Centers for Disease Control and Prevention rates dengue fever and malaria as mosquito-carried diseases having the biggest effect on people.

ENCEPHALITIS

Encephalitis is another virus-caused disease that is sometimes carried by mosquitoes. When the virus organisms travel to a person's brain, that person develops a fever, stiff neck, headache, and nausea. Sometimes, the brain swells and may be damaged. The person may go into a coma or even die.

Aedes and *Culex* mosquitoes are two kinds of mosquitoes that frequently spread encephalitis. You've already seen the stripes that identify *Aedes* mosquitoes. The *Culex* mosquito also has stripes. The *Culex* mosquito has a light band on its dark proboscis.

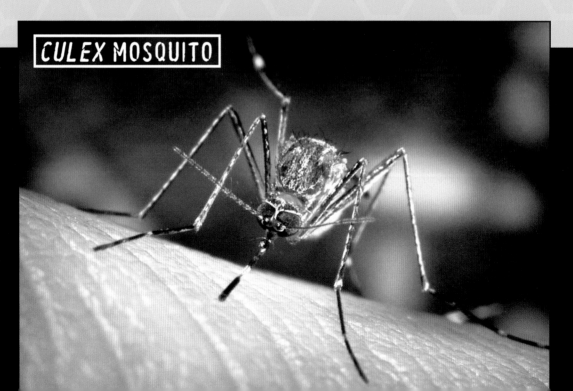

CULEX MOSQUITO

Like *Anopheles, Culex* mosquitoes lay their eggs in water. But their eggs lack wings. *Culex* mosquitoes help their eggs float by sticking them together to form an egg raft. (*See* page 10.) The whole raft is little—only about 0.25 inches (6 millimeters) long and 0.12 inches (3 mm) wide.

Adult *Culex* mosquitoes usually spend their lives close to where they grow up. Some seem to travel farther, though. Scientists have found *Culex* mosquitoes may fly as far as 2 miles (3.22 kilometers). This lets them carry encephalitis to whole new areas.

MOSQUITO FACT

Every year, there are cases of encephalitis reported around the world. Most are in Asia and Australia.

PLACES WHERE ENCEPHALITIS IS FOUND

FIGHTING THE PUBLIC ENEMY

The simplest way people have of controlling mosquito populations is to stop these insects from breeding. The best way to do that is to drain ponds and get rid of places water can collect—even old bottles and tires. After all, the first three stages of a mosquito's life—egg, larva, and pupa—are spent in water. In tropical countries, though, rainy seasons and poor living conditions make it impossible to get rid of all mosquito breeding sites. Then it may be necessary to spray some areas with insecticides, chemicals that kill insects, including mosquitoes.

Sometimes mosquito populations can't be easily controlled. Then people need to protect themselves from mosquito bites. Screens and mosquito nets help. These are both made of fine mesh materials. Air can flow through the mesh, but mosquitoes can't fly through. Mosquito nets are often also treated with insecticides. Then they repel mosquitoes or kill any that land on the net.

MOSQUITO FACT

Repellents keep mosquitoes from biting. These are chemicals mosquitoes sense and avoid. But they only protect whatever they're on. Repellents also have to be reapplied every few hours.

SCREENS

MOSQUITO NETTING

INSECTICIDES

People living where winters are harsh have a natural mosquito control. Most mosquitoes die when the weather turns cold. Low temperatures don't kill all the mosquitoes though. As the weather cools, egg-carrying females of some kinds of mosquitoes, like *Culex* mosquitoes, seek shelter. They crawl into woodpiles, cracks in tree bark, or even inside houses. There they hibernate. Their body functions slow so much that they can survive without feeding. Come spring, the female mosquitoes become active again. They quickly find a body of standing water and lay their eggs. Soon mosquito larvae hatch. With a few months of warm weather, the mosquito population is booming again.

MOSQUITO FACT

Some kinds of mosquitoes, like *Aedes* mosquitoes, stay in the egg stage all through the winter.

Areas that traditionally had cold winters are becoming warmer. So mosquitoes are breeding for longer periods each year. Travel to tropical places has become easier. Travelers may get diseases like malaria and dengue fever. When they return home, they may pass on diseases to local mosquitoes, which then start spreading the illnesses.

Scientists are working to develop vaccines against malaria and other diseases. They are also trying to raise mosquitoes that naturally resist becoming hosts to diseases. But for now, mosquitoes continue to be public enemies, especially in tropical countries. And the battle to find ways to protect people from being bitten by mosquitoes continues.

MOSQUITOES AND OTHER INSECT TROUBLEMAKERS

MOSQUITOES BELONG TO A GROUP, or order, of insects called Diptera (DIP-ter-ra). That name comes from the Greek words for "two" and "wings." Almost all of these insects have only two wings. This group also includes horseflies and houseflies. There are more than 85,000 different kinds of Diptera.

SCIENTISTS GROUP living and extinct animals with others that are similar. So mosquitoes and their kin are classified this way:
Kingdom: Animalia
Phylum: Arthropoda
Class: Insecta
Order: Diptera

HELPFUL OR HARMFUL? Mosquitoes are very harmful because they spread diseases to humans. Their itchy bites are annoying. But mosquitoes are also helpful. They provide food for many insect–eating animals such as frogs, fish, bats, and birds.

HOW BIG ARE *Anopheles* mosquitoes? They have a wingspan of 0.5 inch (1.3 centimeters).

MORE INSECT PUBLIC ENEMIES

Other insects also spread diseases that make people sick. Compare these public enemies to mosquitoes.

Sand flies are only one-third the size of a mosquito. In some places, sand flies may spread a parasite that causes leishmaniasis (leesh-meh-NI-eh-sehs). This disease can cause open sores, fever, weight loss, and liver damage. Sand flies develop through complete metamorphosis. Only the females bite to suck blood to produce eggs. Leishmaniasis is a problem in southern Texas, Central and South America, southern Europe, Asia, the Middle East, and Africa.

Tsetse flies are large biting flies that live in Africa. Both males and females bite people and suck blood meals. The flies spread single-celled parasites called trypanosomes (try-PAN-oh-soomz), which cause African sleeping sickness. This disease makes people weak and causes heart and kidney damage. Infected people are sleepy during the day and restless at night. Tsetse flies develop through complete metamorphosis. But the female holds one egg at a time in her body. The larva hatches there and feeds on a milky material given off by the female's body. The female releases the larva just before it becomes a pupa.

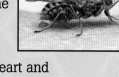

Fleas are wingless, jumping insects. Both adult males and females need blood meals. They feed on both animals and people. Fleas can spread the bubonic plague. Bubonic plague is an infection caused by a kind of bacteria that mainly affects rats. But when the fleas jump from rats to bite people, this disease is spread too. It causes fever, headaches, chills, and blood poisoning. Fleas develop through complete metamorphosis.

GLOSSARY

abdomen: the tail end of an insect. It contains systems for digestion and reproduction.

adult: the final stage of an insect's life cycle

antennae: movable, jointed parts on the insect's head used for sensing

brain: receives messages from the antennae, eyes, and sensory hairs. It sends signals to control all body parts.

complete metamorphosis: a process of development in which the young looks and behaves very differently from the adult. Stages include egg, larva, pupa, and adult.

compound eyes: eyes that are really hundreds of eye units packed together. These let the insect look in every direction at once.

crop: area of digestive system where food is held before it's passed on for further digestion

egg: a female reproductive cell; also the name given to the first stage of an insect's life cycle

esophagus (ee-SAH-feh-gus)**:** a tube through which food passes from the pharynx to the crop or stomach

exoskeleton: protective, skeleton-like covering on the outside of the body

halteres (HAHL-terz)**:** clublike parts in place of hind wings. These help with balance and steering.

head: the insect's body part that has the mouth, the brain, and the sensory organs, such as the eyes and the antennae, if there are any

heart: muscular tube that pumps blood toward the head. Then the blood flows throughout the body.

host: a living animal or plant on which a parasite lives

incomplete metamorphosis: a process of development in which the young look and behave much like a small adult, except that they are unable to reproduce. Stages include egg, nymph, and adult.

intestine (gut): digestion is completed here. Food nutrients pass into the body cavity to enter the blood and flow to all body parts.

larva: the stage between egg and pupa in complete metamorphosis

Malpighian (mal-PEE-gee-an) **tubules:** the organ that cleans the blood and passes wastes to the intestine

molt: the process of an insect shedding its exoskeleton

nerve cord: the nervous system. It sends messages between the brain and other body parts.

nymph: stage between egg and adult in incomplete metamorphosis

ovary (OH-vuh-ree): body part that produces eggs

parasite: living things that live in or on animals or people and get the food they need from their host

pharynx (FAR-ing-ks): tube stretching through the proboscis to the esophagus

proboscis (preh-BAHS-kehs): mouthpart made up of cutting blades and tubes. It is for sucking in blood and plant juices. It also injects saliva.

pupa: stage between larva and adult in complete metamorphosis. At this stage, the larva's body structure and systems are completely changed into its adult form.

rectum: part of digestive system where wastes collect before passing out of the body

salivary gland: produces saliva for digestion. In females, the saliva contains a chemical to keep blood from clotting.

sperm: male reproductive cell

spermatheca (spur-muh-THEE-kuh)**:** sac in female insects that stores sperm after mating

spiracles (SPIR-i-kehlz)**:** holes down the sides of the thorax and abdomen. They let air into and out of the body for breathing.

thorax: the body part between the head and the abdomen. It is where the legs and wings, if there are any, are attached.

virus: tiny organisms that can cause disease

DIGGING DEEPER

To keep on investigating mosquitoes, explore these books and online sites.

BOOKS

DiConsiglio, John. *Blood Suckers!: Deadly Mosquito Bites*. New York: Franklin Watts, 2007. Learn more about the diseases mosquitoes spread.

Morgan, Sally. *Flies and Mosquitoes*. Mankato, MN: Chrysalis Education, 2004. Compare mosquitoes to their cousins, the flies. Look for ways they are alike and how they are different.

Syi, Alexandra, and Dennis Kunkel. *Mosquito Bite*. Watertown, MA: Charlesbridge Press, 2005. See close-up microscopic views of a mosquito throughout its life cycle.

WEBSITES

Mosquitoes—Department of Environmental Protection, Connecticut
http://www.ct.gov/dep/cwp/view.asp?a=2723&q=326190&depNav
_GID=1655
Find out how to stop mosquitoes from breeding near your home. Also take a quiz to learn more mosquito facts.

Mosquito Bytes

http://whyfiles.org/016skeeter
Explore the site to learn more about mosquitoes, including what global warming is likely to mean for this insect and the diseases it transmits.

Tiny Mosquito—Big Trouble

http://www.tinymosquito.com
Explore this website and click on its highlighted words to investigate different species of mosquitoes, the diseases they transmit, how to treat mosquito bites, and lots more.

MOSQUITO ACTIVITIES

GROW MOSQUITO REPELLENT

You like some scents better than others. So do mosquitoes. That's how mosquito repellents work. They have scents mosquitoes avoid. You don't have to buy mosquito repellents. You can grow them. There are plants that naturally keep mosquitoes away. These include marigolds *(right)*, rosemary, catnip, and horsemint. You can buy pots of these plants at your local plant nursery. Or raise them yourself from seeds. You should know a natural repellent has its limits, though. The scent only works at close range. To keep mosquitoes away, you will need to stay close to your potted repellent. Also, each plant only gives off a little bit of scent. So start with at least three pots of natural repellent. Add more as needed to keep mosquitoes away.

SIP THE WAY A MOSQUITO DOES

Mosquitoes have a proboscis, a built-in straw for sucking plant juices and blood. In female mosquitoes, the proboscis has cutting parts to pierce skin. To experience how the mosquito's proboscis works, start with a plastic straw. Use scissors to make a slanted cut across one end of the straw. Trim the straw to a point. Next, pour cranberry juice into a glass. Or use apple juice and add red food coloring to make it blood red. Cover the glass with clear wrap. Stretch the wrap tight. Set the glass in the kitchen sink. Stab the pointed end of the straw straight down onto the clear wrap. Push the straw through the hole it makes. Then sip your pretend blood meal.

INDEX

PHOTO ACKNOWLEDGMENTS

The images in this book are used with the permission of: © TUI DE ROY/Minden Pictures, p. 4; © Dwight R. Kuhn, p. 5; © Warren Photographic, pp. 6–7; © Bill Hauser/Independent Picture Service, pp. 8–9, 21 (bottom), 26, 30 (right), 33; © Kim Taylor/naturepl.com, pp. 10, 39, 41 (middle); © Meul/ARCO/naturepl.com, pp. 11, 37; © NHPA/GEORGE BERNARD, p. 13; © NHPA/ Anthony Bannister, p. 14; © Eye of Science/Photo Researchers, Inc., p. 15; © Lester V. Bergman/ CORBIS, p. 16; © LSHTM/Photo Researchers, Inc., pp. 17, 30 (left); © George Bernard/Photo Researchers, Inc., p. 19; © Gideon Mendel/ActionAid/CORBIS, p. 21 (top); © G. I. Bernard/ Photo Researchers, Inc., p. 23; © Biodisc/Visuals Unlimited, p. 24; © Pascal Goetgheluck/ AUSCAPE, p. 25; © Stephen Dalton/Minden Pictures, p. 27 (both); Centers for Disease Control and Prevention Public Health Image Library, pp. 28, 41 (bottom); © David Kuhn, p. 29; © Nature's Images/Photo Researchers, Inc., p. 31; Centers for Disease Control and Prevention Public Health Image Library/James Gathany, p. 32; © Ariel Skelley/CORBIS, p. 35 (top); © Wendy Stone/ CORBIS, p. 35 (middle); © Rungroj Yongrit/epa/CORBIS, p. 35 (bottom); © Sinclair Stammers/ Photo Researchers, Inc., p. 41 (top); Skip Jeffery Photography, p. 46.

Front Cover: Centers for Disease Control and Prevention Public Health Image Library/ James Gathany.